MW01595612

Study Guide for

# A Virtuous Woman

*By David and Ruth Mast*

**Rod and Staff Publishers, Inc.**
P.O. Box 3, Hwy. 172
Crockett, Kentucky 41413
Telephone: 606-522-4348

Printed in U.S.A.

ISBN 978-07399-2486-0

Catalog no. 21875

1   2   3   4   5   —   24   23   22   21   20   19   18   17   16   15

# Contents

**Chapter 1**

# A Mother's Foundation

## Eternal Father

By faith, I fly beyond all worlds
And see Thee in Thy majesty.
I stand in silence and adore Thee.
This God is the foundation of my life.

Any worthy structure needs a proper foundation to retain its beauty and usefulness. As the weaker vessel, a woman especially needs help to be the kind of woman God wants her to be.

## God

1. Why does a mother need to find a foundation other than herself?

   _____

   _____

2. How is motherhood a calling from God?

   _____

   _____

   _____

3. Why did Manoah want to speak with the man of God?

   _____

   _____

## Her Husband

4. How are husbands foundational?

   _____

   _____

   _____

5. How does a woman's nature differ from that of a man?

_____

_____

_____

## Her Inherent Qualities

6. List some God-given inherent qualities of a mother.

_____

_____

_____

7. In what practical ways do the inherent qualities of a mother manifest themselves?

_____

_____

_____

_____

8. How do a mother's inherent qualities aid her in life?

_____

_____

## Consider further:

If you have failed as a mother, what starting point for recovery does this chapter offer you?

# Chapter 2

# A Mother's Fortification

## Dear Lord and Father of Mankind

Drop Thy still dews of quietness,
Till all our strivings cease;
Take from our souls the strain and stress,
And let our ordered lives confess
The beauty of Thy peace.
—*John G. Whittier*

Because we constantly battle decay in this life, our inner man needs constant renewal and fortification.

## Sincerely Desiring the Word

1. Why is constant fortification so important for a woman?

2. In what way is the Word important in our fortification?

3. What guidelines will help to make devotions effective in a mother's life?

4. What are some things that we should anticipate from our time with God?

## Profitable Thought Life

5. Why is what we think about important?

6. Give some guidelines for maintaining right thoughts.

7. How can we take responsibility for what we think?

8. How can we identify and correct wrong thought patterns?

## A Godly Husband

9. How is a godly husband a wife's fortification?

10. What are some proper responses of a wife to a godly husband's leadership?

## Her Church Family

11. How can a mother prepare for a meaningful church service?

12. What are some helps for receiving inspiration from singing?

13. What are some helps for receiving inspiration from preaching?

14. What are some things that will hinder worship?

15. What are some helps for making baptism and Communion services meaningful to ourselves?

16. In what instances were women involved in worship in the Bible?

17. What benefits do you receive from your church, other than blessings from worship services?

## Reading for Enrichment

18. What kind of reading fortifies?

19. What kind of reading is harmful?

 

 

 

## Guarding Her Health

20. Why should a mother give special attention to her physical and mental health?

 

 

 

 

21. In what ways can you improve and guard your physical and mental health?

 

 

 

 

## Consider further:

Which reminder in this chapter did you need most?

# Chapter 3

# A Mother's Goals for Herself

Setting goals helps a godly woman focus on what is important. Goals channel our thoughts and energy toward a desired object or prize. These goals influence our daily lives.

## "Seek Ye First the Kingdom of God"

1. Why is "loving the Lord with all our heart" such a great commandment?

   _____

   _____

   _____

## "Teach Us to Pray"

2. According to the model of the Lord's Prayer, what should we include in our prayers?

   _____

   _____

   _____

3. How can prayer be helpful when we are tempted?

   _____

   _____

   _____

4. How do we pray in submission and humility?

   _____

   _____

5. How can we pray without ceasing?

   _____

   _____

6. Why do we need prayer as part of our spiritual armor?

_____

_____

## "Rooted and Built Up in Him"

7. What can we do to grow strong in the Christian faith?

_____

_____

_____

8. Why should a woman not depend solely on her husband to know truth and error? What help is there for a godly woman whose husband is spiritually weak?

_____

_____

_____

_____

_____

## "Ponder the Path of Thy Feet"

9. What did Lot's wife have in her heart that made her look back toward Sodom?

_____

_____

_____

10. How or when might we be tempted to look back?

_____

_____

_____

11. What is a straight path, and why is it so important?

_____

_____

_____

## "A Good Name"

12. How can we choose a good name?

_____

_____

13. How can we change the impression that people have of us?

_____

_____

## "He That Ruleth His Spirit"

14. What happens when the enemy controls our spirit?

_____

_____

15. How can we learn self-control?

_____

_____

_____

16. How might we show a lack of self-control in our interactions with others?

_____

_____

_____

17. How might we show intemperance in the way we live?

_____

_____

_____

## "A Merry Heart"

18. What is the basis for a Christian mother's happiness?

_____

_____

_____

19. What are some good ways for a mother to express happiness?

20. Why is your cheerfulness important to your home?

## "Godliness With Contentment"

21. Why did Jesus tell us to "beware of covetousness"?

22. If we are serious about the pilgrim-and-stranger concept, how will it affect our possessions?

23. How should we respond to the many advertisements that present themselves?

24. In what ways does the love of money commonly affect mothers?

## "I Press Toward the Mark"

25. What is involved in pressing toward a goal?

26. What are some past things that we should forget, and why?

_____

_____

_____

## Have a Vision

27. How should we prepare ourselves for service?

_____

_____

28. How can mothers be missionaries for Christ?

_____

_____

_____

29. How can we help our children to have a vision?

_____

_____

_____

## "Labourers Together With God"

30. As a team, how do husband and wife share equal responsibility?

_____

_____

_____

31. What can a wife do to help produce a good working relationship with her husband?

_____

_____

_____

## Some Selfish Goals

32. List some selfish goals that a mother may have.

_____

_____

_____

33. Consider the path you are treading. How can you make it safe for those who follow you?

_____

_____

_____

## Consider further:

Review the headings in this chapter. What goal or goals would you like to make a matter of special prayer and effort?

**Chapter 4**

# A Mother's Adornment

## Let the Beauty of Jesus Be Seen

Let the beauty of Jesus be seen in me,
All His wonderful passion and purity;
May His Spirit divine all my being refine,
Let the beauty of Jesus be seen in me.
—*George L. Johnson*

It does not matter whether you are plain, disfigured, ugly, or attractive. What does matter is the beauty of your heart. The adornment of a meek and quiet spirit will outshine your physical features.

## "Beauty Is Vain"

1. To what extent should we judge a stranger by the appearance of her physical features?

_____

_____

_____

_____

## "In Modest Apparel"

2. Describe a dress that says, "I want to be noticed."

_____

_____

3. What thoughts or feelings are produced by immodest clothing? by modest clothing?

_____

_____

_____

_____

4. Describe a modest dress. How do you feel about wearing one?

_____

_____

_____

5. When does a modest dress become immodest?

_____

_____

6. Why should a Christian woman not arrange her hair in an elaborate manner?

_____

_____

_____

_____

7. How can you be neat and modest at the same time?

_____

_____

## "The Hidden Man of the Heart"

8. What is "the hidden man of the heart"?

_____

_____

9. How can our family tell if we are like a tree by a river?

_____

_____

_____

10. What happens when we neglect our daily Bible reading and prayer?

_____

_____

_____

## "With Good Works"

11. What are some Bible examples of women who were active workers?

    _____

    _____

    _____

*12. Under what conditions is it appropriate to care for an older person in a non-Christian home?

    _____

    _____

13. What are some things you can do for other mothers in the church?

    _____

    _____

14. When are we too busy doing good deeds?

    _____

    _____

## Neatness and Cleanliness

15. Why is it important to be neat and clean? (See 1 Corinthians 6:11, 19, 20.)

    _____

    _____

    _____

    _____

16. What does our appearance on weekdays tell our family about ourselves?

    _____

    _____

    _____

    _____

* A star indicates a discussion question that is not directly answered in the book.

17. Why is cleanliness appropriate for worship?

_____

_____

_____

## Consider further:

Many women are beautiful long after they are finished being pretty. Explain.

# Chapter 5

# A Virtuous Woman

How much are you worth? Would you like to be worth more than a ruby? Then be virtuous!

The following virtues are taken from Proverbs 31. King Lemuel learned about these from his mother. She knew that such an important man as a king needed a wise and virtuous woman by his side. The godly man of today also needs daily help from the kind of woman who is more precious than rubies.

## "Looketh Well to the Ways of Her Household"

1. What makes an attractive home?

   _____

   _____

2. Give some ways that houses reflect the people who live there. Then consider whether your home reflects godly values and how you could improve in this area.

   _____

   _____

   _____

   _____

*3. What are some advantages in having a pleasant breakfast together as a family?

   _____

   _____

   _____

4. What should be done regularly before Father comes home? (Consider: Would you want to come home to a house that looks like yours?)

   _____

   _____

   _____

---

* A star indicates a discussion question that is not directly answered in the book.

## "Worketh Willingly With Her Hands"

5. Why is it honorable to work with your hands?

_____

_____

6. Name some good work habits.

_____

_____

_____

7. What are some practical ways to help children be good and willing workers?

_____

_____

_____

8. What are some ways to lighten your own workload?

_____

_____

_____

9. Why is it important to pay attention to details and teach the same to our children?

_____

_____

_____

10. Why must we plan wisely in order to make balanced use of our time?

_____

_____

_____

## "Bringeth Her Food From Afar"

11. Why is it best to eat at home?

_____

_____

_____

12. What are some pointers for providing good, attractive meals?

_____

_____

_____

13. What are some factors to consider in deciding whether a garden should be a priority?

_____

_____

_____

_____

## "She Is Not Afraid of the Snow"

14. Why is it wise to plan how we will provide clothes for the family?

_____

_____

15. What things should we consider when buying clothes?

_____

_____

_____

16. What can we do if we have a large family and sewing is a major task?

_____

_____

## "A Portion to Her Maidens"

17. In what cases does a mother need extra help?

_____

_____

18. What can you do to make your maid feel comfortable?

_____

_____

_____

19. How should your children interact with the maid?

_____

_____

_____

20. What should be considered in relation to paying a maid?

_____

_____

_____

21. What should you provide if a helper stays at your house for a number of nights?

_____

_____

_____

## "Her Candle Goeth Not Out"

22. What kind of mother is suggested by the burning candle of Proverbs 31?

_____

_____

23. In what practical ways does a mother's presence give security?

_____

_____

_____

## "She Openeth Her Mouth With Wisdom"

24. Why does a Christian mother need special wisdom from God?

_____

_____

25. How can you contribute to your husband's spiritual and material welfare?

_____

_____

_____

26. How can you have a positive influence on your children's attitudes?

_____

_____

_____

27. Define pure speech.

_____

_____

_____

28. When should you hold your tongue?

_____

_____

## "Every Wise Woman Buildeth Her House"

29. How can we help our home to have a good foundation?

_____

_____

_____

30. What are some ways to protect our family from worldly influences?

_____

_____

_____

31. In what way does a mother's teaching illustrate the words "precept upon precept; line upon line"?

_____

_____

_____

32. In what ways might we be like the foolish woman who plucks down her house?

_____

_____

_____

## "A Gracious Woman Retaineth Honour"

33. What features do you think about in the "ideal" gracious woman?

_____

_____

_____

34. What are some illustrations of being a gracious woman in real married life?

_____

_____

_____

35. What are some illustrations of being a gracious woman in relating to children?

_____

_____

_____

_____

36. What other traits does a gracious woman display?

_____

_____

_____

_____

_____

37. How does a gracious woman relate to the good as compared with the excellent?

_____

_____

_____

38. How does a gracious woman retain dignity and reserve?

_____

_____

39. What is meant by the wedding-day honor of a bride? How can a wife tell whether she has retained that honor?

_____
_____
_____
_____
_____

## "A Crown to Her Husband"

40. How might a wife mar her husband's image?

_____
_____

41. How might a wife improve her husband's image?

_____
_____
_____

42. How can you identify with your husband?

_____
_____

## "A Prudent Wife"

43. What is prudence?

_____
_____
_____

44. What are some poor and some good responses to reproof?

_____
_____
_____

45. How can you display prudence in relation to your husband's possessions?

   _____

   _____

   _____

   _____

46. Titus 2:5 says that the aged women should teach the younger women "to be discreet." What does this imply about the older women?

   _____

   _____

47. "A prudent [woman] foreseeth the evil." What potential evil does she see in her children's future, and what does she do to avoid it?

   _____

   _____

   _____

## Consider further:

Some women resent the virtuous woman of Proverbs 31 because she seems to be perfect. How does this study help you to feel more comfortable in striving to be a virtuous woman?

## Watch Your Tone

Our tone of voice gives impressions.
You do not need to say it; they will feel it.
Warm, loving, sunshiny; or cold, hateful, stinging.
One gives healing balm and peace of mind; the other rips and cuts.

**Chapter 6**

# Relating to Her Husband

Our wedding day marks the beginning of what we hope will be a wonderful marriage. How wonderful it is will depend on our choices, especially that of whether we cater to ourselves or to our husbands.

Husband and wife both deal with the carnal nature. How they choose to control this nature determines how happy they will be.

A woman wants to be beautiful and necessary to her husband. Following Bible principles will help her cultivate a beautiful character.

## Respecting His Headship

1. What is the headship order that God outlined in 1 Corinthians 11:3?

   _____

   _____

2. What role does God's headship order give to the man? to the woman?

   _____

   _____

3. What does the headship covering acknowledge? What does this mean for a single woman?

   _____

   _____

   _____

4. In what ways does a faithful wife respect and support her husband behind the scenes?

   _____

   _____

   _____

   _____

## Encouraging Him in His Leadership Role

5. How could a girl's childhood experiences contribute to an overaggressive nature?

_____

_____

_____

6. What can a wife do to encourage leadership in her husband?

_____

_____

_____

7. What aggressive attitudes or actions of a wife might antagonize her husband?

_____

_____

_____

8. How might a wife treat her husband as if he were a boy?

_____

_____

_____

9. How can a wife help her husband in his weak areas?

_____

_____

_____

## Submitting to Him

10. For what reasons might submission be difficult for a new bride?

_____

_____

_____

11. Why is it a great blessing to learn submission as a child?

_____

_____

12. Give some characteristics of true submission.

13. In what practical ways do husbands show love and care for their wives?

14. How should a wife respond to her husband's love and care?

15. How can you show a submissive spirit when you do not agree with your husband's change of plans or his discipline of a child?

## Loving Him

16. Name some things that true love is *not*.

17. Loving your husband is not always spontaneous. Explain.

18. How can you show true love to your husband in words?

19. What are some ways that you can make time to be with your husband?

20. How can you show true love to your husband when he talks to you?

_____

_____

21. How can you show respect for your husband's labors by your spending habits?

_____

_____

_____

22. Name some simple, everyday things you can do to show your husband that you love him.

_____

_____

_____

## Rendering Due Benevolence

23. Your husband is jealous of your love, and you are jealous of his. How does this jealousy protect your marriage?

_____

_____

24. How can we cultivate the exclusive love between husband and wife?

_____

_____

25. What should you do if your thoughts contribute to a poor relationship with your husband?

_____

_____

_____

26. Name virtues that bring satisfaction in marriage.

_____

_____

# As Members of His Body

27. In light of the differing gifts of husband and wife, why is it important that the two become one?

28. In what way should a wife be an extension of her husband?

29. How can you be loyal to your husband in spite of his weaknesses?

30. How can you cause your husband's influence to reach other people?

31. When a wife succeeds in a major project, what can she do to avoid outshining her husband?

32. Name some ways to share in your husband's joys and sorrows.

# Inspiring Trust and Confidence

33. What are some ways that you can build confidence in your marriage?

6. *Relating to Her Husband*

34. What is a good way to deal with a private problem between you and your husband?

_____

_____

_____

35. How can a wife discern whether or not to share a private problem with someone else?

_____

_____

_____

_____

## Contentions of a Wife

36. What actions of a wife will weaken her husband's resolve?

_____

_____

37. In what ways might a wife try to "carve" her husband into a "smaller size"?

_____

_____

_____

38. What are the basic goals of a contentious wife?

_____

_____

39. What is suggested by the phrase "a brawling woman in a wide house"?

_____

_____

## Relating to the Unbelieving Husband

40. According to 1 Corinthians 7:13, how must a believing wife *not* relate to her unbelieving husband?

_____

_____

41. What are some ways in which a Christian husband and an unbelieving husband are alike?

_____

_____

_____

_____

42. How can a wife show that her loyalty to Christ is not a threat to her unbelieving husband?

_____

_____

_____

_____

43. What can a wife do if her husband opposes her attendance at a certain church?

_____

_____

_____

_____

44. How can a wife best work through issues where she differs with her unbelieving husband?

_____

_____

_____

45. How can a wife provide opportunities for family togetherness in spite of any religious differences?

_____

_____

_____

46. What are some ways a wife can help her children have respect for their unbelieving father?

_____

_____

47. What should a wife do instead of concentrating on her unbelieving husband's relationship with God?

_____

_____

_____

_____

48. How can a wife "be blameless and harmless, the [daughter] of God, without rebuke"? (Philippians 2:15).

_____

_____

_____

## Consider further:

Which passage in this chapter, if any, would it be helpful for you to copy and tuck in your Bible?

### ꝩor me to remember . . .

What God hath joined together
Let not man put asunder. . . .
Live in peace; fear God and
keep His commandments. Amen.

# Chapter 7

# A Mother Reaching Out

Did you say you had always wanted to be a missionary? You can be one, right from your front door, or from your mailbox or telephone, or even from your knees.

## Letting Your Light Shine

1. What are some ways that a godly woman can be a witness in her community?

2. How can you display Christian virtues as you interact with your children?

3. To whom does a witness go forth from what they see in your house?

4. What practical things can a godly woman do to be a witness to her neighbors?

5. How can a wife help to be a witness at a foreign mission?

6. How should you respond if a stranger comes to the door and asks for food or shelter?

_____

_____

_____

_____

## Imparting Strength to Those Within

7. What blessings result from providing material assistance to others in the church?

_____

_____

_____

8. Name some simple ways that you can help a sister in the church.

_____

_____

_____

9. How can hospitality be more than just a bed or a meal?

_____

_____

_____

10. What personal direction is it good to pray for at the end of a church service?

_____

_____

_____

11. How can mothers in a new outreach be a blessing to each other?

_____

_____

_____

12. What can you do to make the transition to a Biblical church easier for a mother?

_____

_____

_____

## Helping in the School

13. How can you be a helper in your Christian school?

_____

_____

14. What are some points to remember in relation to mothers teaching classes at school?

_____

_____

_____

15. What are the long-term benefits of showing interest in other people's children?

_____

_____

_____

## Nurturing the Seeking Soul

16. Why is it best to communicate face to face with a seeking soul? What are some other acceptable ways?

_____

_____

_____

17. How should a woman respond if a man at the grocery store asks for spiritual help?

_____

_____

_____

18.  How does witnessing to others affect our own Christian life?

_____

_____

_____

## Consider further:

As you contemplate reaching out to others, whose name comes to your mind first?

Inasmuch as ye have done it
unto one of the least of these my brethren,
ye have done it unto me.
Matthew 25:40

# Chapter 8

# Problems Mothers Face

## Fear

Fear is a strong, unpleasant emotion caused by the anticipation of danger. Fear makes us despondent and moody, and it colors our decisions.

1. What are some common causes of fear?

2. Why does unconfessed sin bring fear?

3. How can we help our children to cope with fear?

4. Fear comes when our focus is not on God. Explain.

5. How is open communication with other sisters in the church a help in combating fear?

6. List some Scripture verses that are helpful to you when you are afraid.

7. How did prayer help Daniel when he faced the threat of the den of lions?

_____
_____
_____

## Worry and Anxiety

Worry and anxiety are closely related to the emotion of fear. They reveal a lack of trust in God. We are plagued with "what if's." The enemy uses our imagination to trouble us.

8. What is something helpful to remember when we have worries based on imagination?

_____
_____
_____

9. What are some things we can do when we are tempted to worry?

_____
_____
_____

10. When is worry based on pride or selfishness?

_____
_____
_____

11. What should you do with worries about things that you can help? about things you cannot help?

_____
_____
_____

12. What is the difference between worry and proper concern?

_____
_____

13. Why is it generally a sin to worry?

_____
_____
_____

# Doubt (Lack of Assurance of Salvation)

Assurance of salvation brings joy and peace to our lives, enabling us to communicate freely with God. Every Christian needs this assurance to live in victory. Satan uses the tool of doubt very effectively to disturb our connection with God.

14. List some Scripture verses that say we can have assurance of salvation.

_____

_____

15. How might another person's testimony cause us to doubt our salvation? How can we avoid this trap?

_____

_____

_____

16. Answer the following questions, using the points under "Helps From 1 John."

    a. What is a good way to tell that we are walking in the light?

    _____

    _____

    b. We confess our sins when we receive salvation. What must we do if we sin later?

    _____

    _____

    _____

    c. What is a clear indication of not being a child of God?

    _____

    _____

    d. What are some indications of love for the world?

    _____

    _____

    e. How does a true Christian seek to live? How does he seek not to live?

    _____

    _____

    _____

    f.  What does it take to have a clear conscience, one that is confident in facing God?

_____

_____

_____

    g.  What will help us to continue loving a brother in spite of his thoughtlessness?

_____

_____

_____

    h.  What two things are included in confessing that Jesus is the Son of God?

_____

_____

_____

17.  Why is it unwise or even dangerous to depend on feelings as proof of whether we are saved?

_____

_____

_____

18.  How do feelings relate to facts and faith?

_____

_____

19.  Some people think that once they have received Christ as their Saviour, they cannot fall from grace. What evidence in the Bible shows that this is a false idea?

_____

_____

_____

# Gossip

    Our little member the tongue is a powerful tool. This member can be either a blessing or a curse, depending on what we say and how we say it.

20. Give a brief description of each kind of person.

gossip _____

_____

talebearer _____

_____

whisperer _____

_____

tattler _____

_____

busybody _____

_____

21. How could we become the instigator of a division in the brotherhood?

_____

_____

22. How can gossip damage our Christian witness?

_____

_____

23. "Behold, how great a matter a little fire kindleth!" Why is this a fitting description of gossip?

_____

_____

_____

24. What are the results if a wife shares her husband's confidential matters with others?

_____

_____

_____

25. In speaking of a person, what should we do instead of making things sound as bad as we can?

_____

_____

_____

26. Whom is it proper to tell about an offense? Whom is it not proper to tell?

27. What are some questions that will help us decide whether to say a certain thing about a person?

28. What is a good way to overcome the urge to gossip about someone?

## Inferior or Superior Feelings

Everyone deals with inferior or superior feelings. God does not want us to have either of them.

29. How will a proper view of God affect our attitude toward ourselves?

30. How did Queen Esther show that she had a proper attitude toward herself?

31. How did King Nebuchadnezzar show that he had an improper attitude toward himself?

32. What are some common excuses for refusing to enter into the Lord's work?

33. Why do we sometimes hide our God-given talents and abilities?

_____

_____

34. How should we relate to the gifts of others in the church? to our own gifts?

_____

_____

_____

_____

35. What will cause us to come short of God's measure?

_____

_____

## Self-pity

Self-pity brings an emotional release to a selfish attitude. Because of a real or imagined wrong done to us, we feel justified in our pity party and actually enjoy feeling sorry for ourselves.

36. What causes self-pity? What are its effects within us?

_____

_____

_____

_____

37. What are some childish expressions of self-pity?

_____

_____

38. Why is self-pity so deceptive?

_____

_____

39. How might others suffer because of self-pity in a mother?

_____

_____

40. What are some greater evils that often follow self-pity?

_____

_____

41. What are some good things to do when we are tempted to feel sorry for ourselves?

_____

_____

_____

42. When is self-pity not entirely a spiritual problem? What will help to relieve this problem?

_____

_____

_____

## Jealousy

There are two kinds of jealousy. The proper kind guards the love between husband and wife, and between God and us. The wrong kind is associated with rivalry, envy, suspicion, strife, and similar works of the flesh.

43. In what ways does God reveal His jealous love for us?

_____

_____

44. How does this same kind of jealousy protect a marriage?

_____

_____

45. In what sense is a spiritual shepherd rightly jealous for his flock?

_____

_____

46. Describe jealousy of the wrong kind.

_____

_____

47. What are some causes of jealousy in mothers?

_____

_____

_____

48. Why should you be careful about a close friendship with someone other than your husband?

_____

_____

_____

49. How might we show the wrong kind of jealousy when our children appreciate other adults in the church? Why is this harmful?

_____

_____

50. What should we do when wrong feelings of jealousy arise within us?

_____

_____

## Consider further:

What problem or problems in this chapter do you remember striving with and overcoming? How did you do it?

> Sister, are you weary?
> Do you lack motivation?
> Are you distressed?
> "Come to Me," saith One,
> "And, coming, be at rest."
> —*Stephen, the Sabaite*

## Chapter 9

# Building Sound Family Life

Everyone enjoys being part of a happy, contented family. Happy families are made; they do not just happen. Christian fathers and mothers seek to do what is needed to bring happiness and harmony to their home.

## Observing God's Order of Headship

1. Why did God establish a headship order?

_____

_____

2. What is the most important thing for a wife to do as the "copilot" in her home?

_____

_____

_____

3. What happens when a wife interferes with her husband's directions?

_____

_____

4. Why is it important for you to abide by the same rules, whether or not your husband is home?

_____

_____

_____

## Worship in the Home

5. What does family worship do for our children?

_____

_____

6. When we tell Bible stories to children, what do they learn beyond the events in the stories?

_____

_____

_____

7. How can we teach our children that the Bible is our source of direction for life?

_____

_____

8. What are some pointers for singing in family worship?

_____

_____

_____

9. What are some pointers for prayer in family worship?

_____

_____

_____

10. When might our family worship be a witness to others?

_____

_____

_____

_____

11. What are some guidelines for family worship when no father is present to lead out?

_____

_____

_____

## The Church Contributing to Our Family Life

12. What are some spiritual benefits that the church provides for our families?

_____

_____

_____

13. As parents, how does our church membership contribute to our family's well-being?

   _____

   _____

   _____

   _____

   _____

14. In relation to the church, why does it matter what happens in our homes?

   _____

   _____

   _____

15. What are some specific ways to make family plans revolve around church functions?

   _____

   _____

   _____

   _____

16. How should we respond to a financial need in the church? What effect does our response have on our children?

   _____

   _____

   _____

17. How can we help our children to have good attitudes and a sense of responsibility toward the church?

   _____

   _____

18. How can we teach our children the importance of blending with the brotherhood?

   _____

   _____

   _____

# Hospitality

19. What is involved in hospitality?

_____

_____

_____

20. What are some rewards of showing hospitality to a family of strangers?

_____

_____

_____

21. What benefits do our children receive when we have guests in our home?

_____

_____

_____

# Good Literature

22. Why must we be careful about the books we choose for our family?

_____

_____

_____

23. What do we gain from good reading materials?

_____

_____

_____

24. What are some clues that reading has become an obsession?

_____

_____

25. How can we help small children to develop an interest in books?

_____

_____

_____

26. How can we get our children to read (especially heavier material) if they do not enjoy it?

_____

_____

_____

## Christian Schools

27. How does the Christian school strengthen the Christian home?

_____

_____

28. What view of a Christian school will help us to have a right attitude about the sacrifice and expense involved?

_____

_____

29. How should we relate to the teachers, the school board, and the ministry as they direct the school?

_____

_____

30. How can we show our children that we expect them to be diligent in school?

_____

_____

31. How is school a blessing in relation to the weak spots of parents?

_____

_____

_____

32. What are some ways to show interest in our children's school lessons and activities?

_____

_____

33. In what ways does the school prepare our children for adult life?

_____

_____

# The Pilgrim-and-Stranger Concept

34. How should we look at our possessions and at ourselves in relation to them?

35. What is the pilgrim-and-stranger concept?

36. What lessons can we learn from the pilgrim journey of Abraham's wife Sarah?

37. How can we tell whether earthly possessions are too dear to us?

38. What are some attitudes that reveal a pilgrim's view of earthly possessions?

# Appreciation for Our Heritage

39. Why is it important for us to know historical facts like those recorded in Hebrews 11:35–38?

40. What is a wrong way to relate to a godly heritage? Whom did Jesus rebuke for doing this?

41. How can we best show appreciation for a godly heritage?

_____

_____

_____

42. What concerns should we have in relation to a child who wants to be baptized?

_____

_____

_____

_____

43. What are some benefits of a true appreciation for our Christian heritage?

_____

_____

_____

## Working Together

44. Why is it important for a child to share the workload of the family?

_____

_____

45. What purpose for learning to work extends beyond the need to get the job done?

_____

_____

_____

46. Why do children need supervision in their work, especially at first?

_____

_____

_____

47. How can we help a child to be responsible in his work? to develop confidence in his work?

_____

_____

_____

48. What are some benefits of hobbies and special-interest projects?

_____

_____

_____

## Disciplined Lifestyle

49. What are some features of a disciplined lifestyle?

_____

_____

50. In what ways is a disciplined lifestyle healthy for children?

_____

_____

_____

51. In what sense does a disciplined lifestyle depend largely on the mother?

_____

_____

_____

52. What are some practical pointers for helping a mother to get things done on time?

_____

_____

_____

53. What are some practical areas in which our example of discipline influences our children?

_____

_____

54. How should we relate to interruptions in our schedule?

_____

_____

## Consider further:

Which of the good habits mentioned in this chapter have you admired in others?

# Chapter 10

# Relationships That Build Sound Family Life

> I shall live on in the lives of my children,
> Whether for good or ill,
> Long, long after my voice that is speaking
> Today, is still.
>
> —*Grace Noll Crowell*

## Respect

1. How can we teach a proper respect for God to very young children? to older children?

   _____
   _____
   _____
   _____

2. How can we show respect for ministers and fellow members in the church?

   _____
   _____

3. What are some ways that we can "honour the king"?

   _____
   _____

4. How should we honor and respect our parents if they are Christians? if they are not Christians?

   _____
   _____
   _____
   _____

5. What are some ways that children should show respect to each other?

   _____

   _____

   _____

6. What are some things that different mothers do differently? How do we help our children when we show tolerance toward other people's ways of doing things?

   _____

   _____

   _____

## Love and Forbearance

7. Give some human tendencies that make love and forbearance necessary in family life.

   _____

   _____

   _____

   _____

8. When should love cover a multitude of our children's faults? What are the limits of forbearance, such as when a six-year-old daughter chews celery with her mouth open?

   _____

   _____

   _____

   _____

9. How should we deal with our children's tendency to retaliate?

   _____

   _____

   _____

10. What are some evidences of a critical spirit? How should we deal with it in our children?

   _____

   _____

   _____

11. What are some good ways to respond when we are wrongfully accused?

_____

_____

_____

## Kindness and Courtesy

12. Is it true that home is the place to be free to act as we wish? Explain.

_____

_____

_____

13. In what ways can we provide good examples of courtesy for our children?

_____

_____

_____

14. How can we help our children find joy and satisfaction in putting others first?

_____

_____

_____

15. Why is it hard to practice the Golden Rule? Why must we not neglect it in the home?

_____

_____

_____

16. What is involved in truly forgiving?

_____

_____

_____

## Trust and Confidence

17. What qualities of Abraham and Isaac's relationship are evident in their experience at Mount Moriah?

_____

_____

18. How can mothers inspire their children to trust in God?

_____

_____

19. How can we build our children's confidence in ourselves as mothers?

_____

_____

_____

20. How can we build our children's trust in our advice and counsel?

_____

_____

_____

21. What basic confidence must our children have in us?

_____

_____

22. What will harm or destroy our children's confidence in us?

_____

_____

## Communication

23. Why is it good to tell our children about our plans for the day?

_____

_____

_____

24. What is the value of expressing appreciation to our children for work well done?

_____

_____

_____

25. What are the benefits of making good connections in
    a. giving clear commands and directions? _____

    _____

    _____

    b.  communicating love and concern? _____

_____

_____

_____

26. What are some signs of good connections between parents and adult children living at home?

_____

_____

_____

27. What are some circumstances that require "special connections" for good communication?

_____

_____

28. What are some forms of "static" that hinder communication?

_____

_____

## Togetherness

29. Togetherness refers mainly to what?

_____

_____

_____

30. How can you promote profitable conversations at mealtime?

_____

_____

_____

31. What are some good things for the family to do together at any time? in winter? in summer?

_____

_____

_____

_____

_____

32. What are some good ways for mothers and little children to work together?

_____

_____

_____

## Happiness and Unselfishness

33. How can you teach your child to "love [his] neighbour as [himself]"?

_____

_____

34. In assigning unpleasant work to children, what must a mother guard against? What would be better to do instead?

_____

_____

_____

35. How can a child be happy while doing a chore like washing dishes?

_____

_____

## Family-to-Family Sharing

36. Sharing between families in a congregation should be based on what Christian principles?

_____

_____

_____

37. What are some practical ways to share with other families in the church?

_____

_____

_____

38. What should we do beyond just getting together to have a good time?

_____

_____

_____

## Consider further:

In what specific ways can you work with your husband in promoting the values discussed in this chapter? Likewise, how can you work with your children?

**Chapter 11**

# Hindrances to Sound Family Life

And if a house be divided against itself,
that house cannot stand.
Mark 3:25

## Worldly Amusements

1. Why are radio, television, videos, and the Internet a danger to the Christian family?

2. What are several reasons that computer games are a hindrance to the family?

3. What are some Scriptures that teach us to avoid temptations of the flesh?

## Unsound Literature

4. What will give us the ability to identify unsound reading material?

5. How can we help our children to be "simple concerning evil"?

_____

_____

_____

6. Give some examples of so-called Christian literature that is harmful to read.

_____

_____

_____

7. Why is it important that the traits of story characters be noble and upright?

_____

_____

_____

## Public Schools

8. Why is it unbiblical for strangers and pilgrims to have their children taught in public schools?

_____

_____

_____

9. What things do public schools teach that run counter to Bible principles?

_____

_____

10. What aspects of the public school environment are not conducive to good moral and spiritual development?

_____

_____

_____

## Overmuch Contact With the Apostate and Ungodly

11. What was God's chief concern for Israel in the land of Canaan?

12. What instructions did God give to help Israel remain faithful?

13. What happened to Solomon after he married heathen wives? What lesson can we learn from his experience?

14. What is the danger of freely associating with worldly relatives, friends, and neighbors?

15. How can we maintain a safe position for our family and still express love for lost souls?

## The Going-away Mentality

16. Describe the going-away mentality and the feeling that goes with it.

17. Why is the going-away mentality detrimental to family life?

18. How can a mother influence her children to be content with staying at home?

_____

_____

_____

## Disagreements, Arguments, and Misunderstandings

19. What are some common reasons that a wife opposes her husband?

_____

_____

20. Though disagreements will come, what should a wife carefully avoid?

_____

_____

_____

21. What should you consider if you find yourself in continual disagreement with your husband?

_____

_____

22. What negative effects does it have on children when parents habitually disagree and argue with each other?

_____

_____

_____

## Materialism

23. Covetousness may cause people to do things that are not even logical. How is this illustrated in Achan's case?

_____

_____

_____

24. What are some things we are tempted to covet today?

_____

_____

_____

25. What are some signs of a materialistic attitude?

_____

_____

_____

26. When does materialism cause family life to suffer?

_____

_____

_____

_____

## An Undisciplined Lifestyle

27. What is meant by an undisciplined lifestyle? What are some signs of it?

_____

_____

_____

28. How does laxity in child training contribute to disorder in a home?

_____

_____

_____

29. Why does a lack of routine bring insecurity to children? How can this be remedied?

_____

_____

_____

30. How can you make good intentions work for you?

_____

_____

## Consider further:

Of the statements in this chapter,
- which ones do you need to consider further?
- which ones are you not sure that you agree with?

# Chapter 12

# Goals for Our Children

**Goal for my son:**
That he may be strong in the faith and join hands with the other faithful brethren in the church.

**Goal for my daughter:**
That she may be a worthy example of the Christian faith, living a life that is becoming to a woman professing godliness.

## Fear the Lord

1. How does fear of the Lord develop in a growing child?

   _____

   _____

2. How can parents help to counter peer pressure in a child's life?

   _____

   _____

## Obey Parents

3. What responsibility grows out of the fact that we are responsible for our children's existence?

   _____

   _____

   _____

4. For what two Biblical reasons should our children obey us?

   _____

   _____

   _____

5. What do children learn about God's order of headship when they learn obedience?

_____

_____

_____

## Daniel Purposed in His Heart

6. Through what circumstances were Daniel and his three friends tempted to give up their allegiance to God?

_____

_____

_____

7. How did God bless the unwavering faithfulness of these young men?

_____

_____

8. What are some ways that our children will be tempted in the evil and deceptive days in which they live?

_____

_____

_____

_____

9. How can we as mothers stand between our children and evil influences?

_____

_____

## Self-control

10. What is a good way to help our children learn to control their emotions?

_____

_____

_____

11. How can we teach our children self-control in eating?

_____

_____

_____

12. Contrast a child who is taught to work with one who is allowed to play most of the time.

_____

_____

_____

13. What actions of a little child show that he is old enough to be restrained? What will happen if his parents do not restrain him?

_____

_____

_____

## "A Pattern of Good Works"

14. What is included in "denying ungodliness and worldly lusts"?

_____

_____

_____

15. How is the "blessed hope" a help to the Christian?

_____

_____

_____

16. What are some ways to "drive stakes" that help a child to grow in the right direction?

_____

_____

_____

17. What adjustments may you need to make as your child grows older, to help him fit the pattern you choose?

_____

_____

_____

## "Keep Thyself Pure"

18. In guarding our children's purity, what three important goals should we have for them?

_____

_____

_____

*19. Discuss how purity in the home is affected by each of the following: proper reserve between boys and girls, dress habits, bathroom rules, general supervision

_____

_____

_____

_____

_____

## "He Shall Be Lent to the Lord"

20. Why is a hunter careful about how he fashions his arrows?

_____

_____

_____

_____

_____

21. After children leave home, how are they like arrows that leave a bow?

_____

_____

22. In what ways can you prepare your children for usefulness in serving the Lord?

_____

_____

## "In Thee Also"

23. How did Hezekiah reveal that he had shallow and selfish motives?

_____

_____

_____

_____

24. What is encouraging about the example of Timothy?

_____

_____

_____

25. Why do parents experience joy when their children embrace the faith?

_____

_____

_____

_____

## Some Selfish Goals

26. What are some selfish goals that a mother may have for her children?

_____

_____

_____

27. What are some undesirable results of these goals?

_____

_____

_____

_____

_____

## Consider further:

How does this chapter illustrate the principle that succeeding at secondary goals can prevent us from succeeding where it really matters?

# Chapter 13

# Proper Attitudes Toward Children

Lo, children are an heritage of the LORD:
and the fruit of the womb is his reward.
Psalm 127:3

1. How do you feel about the following attitudes regarding children?

   a. Children are a gift from God. _____

   _____

   _____

   b. Children will further my goals and aspirations. _____

   _____

   _____

   c. Children will take care of me when I am old. _____

   _____

   _____

   d. Children are undying souls to teach and train for God. _____

   _____

   _____

   e. We need a son to carry on the family name. _____

   _____

   _____

   f. Children can help pay off our property debt. _____

   _____

   _____

   g. Children are gifts that I can take along to heaven. _____

   _____

   _____

   h. Children can help us extend the kingdom of Christ. _____

   _____

   _____

2. What words in the Book of Jonah suggest God's regard for children?

 

 

3. What are some benefits of asking God to give us children?

 

 

4. "Be it unto me according to thy word" (Luke 1:38). How does this attitude help a busy, expectant mother?

 

 

 

5. How can a woman find fulfillment when she has been denied children?

 

 

 

6. For what reasons should we have an attitude of joy regarding our children?

 

 

 

 

7. In relation to Christ's kingdom, what important attitude should we have toward children?

 

 

 

## Consider further:

How has reading this chapter affected your view of children?

# Chapter 14

# Meeting the Needs of Our Children

It isn't looks that make one great,
But character that seals our fate.
It's what's within your heart, you see,
That makes or mars your destiny,
And that does really matter.

## Teaching Them About God

1. We cannot see God. Then how can we teach our children about Him?

2. What are some things that children need to know about God?

3. How can we nurture a child's faith in God?

4. Give some examples of everyday activities that we can use to teach our children about God.

5. How can we convey to our children that God always gives what is best for us?

## Their Need to Love and Be Loved

6. What lessons about mothering do older women commonly want younger women to learn?

_____

_____

_____

_____

7. What is meant by having a spiritual love for our children?

_____

_____

_____

8. What kinds of shelter should our love provide?

_____

_____

9. How can we help a child to associate a spanking with love?

_____

_____

_____

10. What are some beneficial results of proper discipline?

_____

_____

## Their Need of Security

11. What are some ways to help a child feel secure in our love?

_____

_____

_____

12. How does your love for your husband provide security for your child?

_____

_____

_____

13. What is the best material security we can give to our children?

_____

_____

_____

14. What is the connection between rules and children's security?

_____

_____

## Their Need for Acceptance and Approval

15. In what ways may we be tempted to show partiality toward our children?

_____

_____

_____

16. How does a child benefit from living with approval?

_____

_____

17. What are the likely results if we inflate our children's egos?

_____

_____

_____

18. What are the likely results if we are too demanding of our children?

_____

_____

19. If a child often does things to get our attention and approval, what may be the reason?

_____

_____

_____

## Their Need for Work and Play

20. What is the danger of allowing a child to do nothing but play?

_____

_____

21. What are some creative ways for children to keep busy?

_____

_____

22. If our standard of perfection is too high, what effect will it have on our children?

_____

_____

_____

23. What are some ways of motivating our children to work?

_____

_____

_____

24. How does play help to prepare a child for life?

_____

_____

_____

25. Why should older children spend less time in play than younger children?

_____

_____

_____

26. What wholesome activities can parents do with their children and teenagers to have enjoyable family diversions?

_____

_____

_____

27. When are diversions overdone?

_____

_____

_____

## Consider further:

What suggestions in this chapter will you use today? tomorrow?

# Chapter 15

# Training and Disciplining Our Children

But the word of the LORD was unto them
precept upon precept, precept upon precept;
line upon line, line upon line;
here a little, and there a little.
Isaiah 28:13

## Our Responsibility and Accountability

1. What is wrong with the idea of training a child in the way he wants to go?

2. What may be the reason that 1 Timothy 5:14 commands mothers to "guide the house"? What are the implications of this command?

3. What Scriptures show that parents are accountable for the actions of their children?

4. Why should parents not ask young children to apologize to God for wrongdoing?

## The Principle of Parental Authority

5. From whom do parents get the authority to discipline their children? Besides giving correction for wrongdoing, what are some practical ways in which parents should exercise their authority?

_____

_____

_____

6. Why are parents the ones best qualified to exercise authority in the home?

_____

_____

_____

_____

7. How do parents become their young children's heroes? How can they maintain that hero image?

_____

_____

_____

8. How might a child try to manipulate his parents? How does manipulation affect parental authority?

_____

_____

_____

9. How is respect for parental authority a benefit to children?

_____

_____

## The Principle of Parental Love

10. How does godly love provide the courage to take even the hardest disciplinary action?

_____

_____

_____

11.  What are some common expressions of mere sentimental love?

_____

_____

## The Principle of the Fallen Nature in the Child

12.  How does a child display the carnal nature?

_____

_____

_____

13.  How does a child feel after doing wrong? What important thing does punishment do for him?

_____

_____

_____

14.  How can you assure your child that you have forgiven his wrong? How does this relate to his later sense of God's forgiveness?

_____

_____

_____

## The Principle of Training the Child

15.  When can we rightly say that our child has been trained?

_____

_____

16.  When is the right time to train a child? Why is that the best time?

_____

_____

17.  What are some practical pointers for training a child?

_____

_____

_____

18. What is meant by manipulating a child? Why is this not an effective training method?

_____

_____

_____

_____

19. What are the only things we should ask of a child? How should we expect him to respond?

_____

_____

_____

## The Principle of Discipline

20. When should children's discipline begin? Why?

_____

_____

_____

21. What kind of discipline is assumed in the verse "If thou beatest him with the rod, he shall not die"?

_____

_____

22. What are some blessings that a properly disciplined child enjoys?

_____

_____

_____

23. What rewards will parents enjoy for properly disciplining their children?

_____

_____

_____

_____

24. How does disciplining our children prepare them for later life?

_____

_____

_____

## The Principle of Molding the Will

25. When does the battle of molding a child's will begin? What are some evidences that the battle has begun?

_____

_____

_____

_____

26. When a child suffers a legitimate hurt, what expressions are proper? improper?

_____

_____

_____

27. What are some practical pointers for molding a young child's will?

_____

_____

_____

28. When is it evident that our molding has been effective?

_____

_____

_____

## "Children's Children Are the Crown"

29. What happens sometimes when a mother yields to weariness and discouragement?

_____

_____

_____

30. What are some pointers for victory in discouraging times?

_____

_____

_____

31. What consequences can we expect if we give up in child training?

_____

_____

32. What rewards can we anticipate for faithfulness in child training?

_____

_____

_____

## Consider further:

In your view, how can you mold a child's will without breaking it?

# Chapter 16

# Child-rearing Challenges

A mother's goal is to help her husband train their children in such a way that they can grow up and be useful to God in His kingdom. This is a very worthy goal; but as is common with all things in life, obstacles present themselves to thwart our efforts. How can a mother turn these obstacles into something good?

## Complaining, Whining, Pouting

1. When should we show extra compassion to a complaining child? When should we not?

   _____

   _____

   _____

2. What do children need to learn about complaining, whining, and pouting?

   _____

   _____

   _____

3. What are some causes of pouting?

   _____

   _____

4. What do children need to learn about pleasing others?

   _____

   _____

## Arguments and Disagreements

5. What do children commonly argue over? What is the motive behind arguing?

   _____

   _____

   _____

6. What preventive measure by parents will reduce arguments and disagreements? What should be promoted instead of strife?

_____

_____

7. What attitude helps to settle arguments? How can we teach it to a child?

_____

_____

_____

8. What kind of discussion is profitable? When is it time to end a discussion?

_____

_____

_____

## Disrespect

9. What is the nature of disrespect?

_____

_____

_____

10. What are some expressions of disrespect?

_____

_____

11. How should we deal with a child who tells his teacher, "You are not my boss"?

_____

_____

_____

12. Why is it crucial that we deal with disrespect when we see it in our young children?

_____

_____

_____

## Retaliation

13. Why should parents teach their children to "resist not evil"?

_____

_____

14. What are some ways to teach nonresistance to our children?

_____

_____

_____

_____

## Showing Off

15. When is it proper to enjoy our little children's antics? What should we do if they continue?

_____

_____

_____

16. What is a proper way for children to behave in the presence of adults?

_____

_____

_____

17. What should we do if our children misbehave in public or when guests are present?

_____

_____

_____

18. Why should we be careful about our response to the antics of other people's children?

_____

_____

_____

# Lying

19. How can we help a child to discern between what is real and what is imaginary?

    _____

    _____

    _____

20. Why should we be careful about accusing little children of lying?

    _____

    _____

21. What signs suggest that a child is lying? Why should we not ask a child whether he did a certain misdeed, when we already know that he is guilty?

    _____

    _____

    _____

22. How can we teach our children to be honest?

    _____

    _____

    _____

# Jealousy and Rivalry

23. What can we do to develop a feeling of oneness in our family?

    _____

    _____

    _____

24. What are some results when parents show favoritism and partiality toward certain of their children?

    _____

    _____

    _____

25. How can we help a two-year-old to deal with feelings of rivalry when a new baby comes?

_____

_____

_____

26. How might we tend to be partial with our children? On the other hand, how can we deal with the fact that it is impossible to make everything fair and equal?

_____

_____

_____

_____

_____

27. What will happen if we encourage a child in the feeling that he is at a disadvantage? What should we do instead?

_____

_____

_____

_____

_____

## Consider further:

Of the challenges discussed in this chapter, which ones should we be especially careful to approach with moderation and consideration for our children?

> Let every one of us please his neighbour
> for his good to edification.
> Romans 15:2

# Chapter 17

# Relating to Our Teenagers

The teen years bring special challenges as well as special blessings. We face continual challenges as we see potential problems and try to avert them or guide our teenagers through them. Blessings come when we freely share our joys and trials. To see our teenagers enjoying a victorious Christian life and fitting into the life of the home and church is every godly parent's aspiration.

## Spiritual Maturity Keeping Pace

1. Why do teenagers question things that they had always accepted before? What opportunity does this provide?

   _____

   _____

   _____

2. Because of new physical feelings and drives, what special temptations do our teenagers face? How can we help them to withstand these temptations?

   _____

   _____

   _____

   _____

   _____

   _____

3. What can we do if spiritual maturity is lacking in our teenagers?

   _____

   _____

   _____

## A Prime Time to Decide for Christ

4. What is a good motive for desiring that a teenager become a Christian?

   _____

   _____

5. How can we prepare our children for the time when the Lord speaks to them?

   _____

   _____

   _____

   _____

6. When a child is troubled in spirit, how can we tell whether it results from his own fears or from the work of the Holy Spirit?

   _____

   _____

7. Some teenagers readily talk about spiritual things, while others are more withdrawn. How should we relate to both of these?

   _____

   _____

## Habits and Attitudes Solidify

8. In nurturing a tree and in raising children, what common human weakness often leads to undesirable results?

   _____

   _____

9. What fruits in a teenager show that our child training has been effective?

   _____

   _____

10. What fruits in a teenager show that our child training has not been effective? What can we do even now to correct the problem?

    _____

    _____

    _____

## Appreciation for Home and Church

11. Teenagers often think they know better than their elders. What will good parents have been doing through the childhood years that will enable them to help their teenagers?

_____

_____

_____

12. In what ways can teenagers contribute to the church? Why are they better suited for some of these things than married people are?

_____

_____

_____

13. How do teenagers develop convictions that are an asset to the church?

_____

_____

_____

## Vulnerability to Their Environment

14. Why must our homes, churches, and schools all speak in a united voice?

_____

_____

_____

15. Drinking, smoking, and ungodly music are obvious sources of defilement. What common sources of defilement are more subtle?

_____

_____

_____

16. What long-term harm may result from defilement in the teen years?

_____

_____

_____

## Interest in the Opposite Gender

17. What should we encourage our teenagers to do instead of feeding an interest in the opposite gender?

_____

_____

_____

18. Describe a proper relationship between teenage boys and girls, in contrast to an improper relationship.

_____

_____

_____

19. What harm is done when a teenager has a special friend of the opposite gender while too young?

_____

_____

_____

## Social Interests

20. If our teenagers *are* true friends and *have* true friends, what will they do for each other?

_____

_____

_____

_____

21. What are some effects of positive and negative peer pressure?

_____

_____

_____

22. How can we warn our teenagers against bad company without belittling others?

_____

_____

_____

23. What can we do so that our homes provide for the social interests of our teenagers?

_____

_____

_____

## Communicating True Love

24. What are some expressions of spiritual love for our teenagers?

_____

_____

_____

25. What are some ways to spend meaningful time with our teenage sons and daughters?

_____

_____

_____

26. How can we show true love for our teenager's soul?

_____

_____

_____

27. How should we respond when a teenager shares a serious personal problem?

_____

_____

_____

## Consider further:

If you have teenagers, how do their trials and triumphs compare with those in your own teenage experience?

And, ye fathers,
provoke not your children to wrath:
but bring them up
in the nurture and admonition of the Lord.
Ephesians 6:4

## Chapter 18

# Relating to Our Daughters

The baby girl in your arms is a living soul in a mortal body. So is your teenage daughter sitting across from you at the table. They will continue to live through time and eternity, forever and ever. God gave you your daughters to prepare them for life and for eternity.

Make your years with your daughters a special time—a time to learn about God and how we are to respond to Him.

## Developing a Meek and Quiet Spirit

1. Describe a meek and quiet spirit.

   _____

   _____

   _____

2. What is the source of a meek and quiet spirit?

   _____

   _____

3. What training can we give our young daughters so that they have a meek and quiet spirit when they become Christians?

   _____

   _____

   _____

4. In what ways should a daughter show respect for her father? How does her mother contribute to that respect?

   _____

   _____

   _____

5. As a mother, what should you do if a daughter grumbles about a command that Father gives?

   _____

   _____

6. What will happen if a daughter shows less than a meek and quiet spirit, but her mother says nothing about it?

_____

_____

7. What does public exposure tend to produce in our daughters, instead of a meek and quiet spirit?

_____

_____

_____

_____

8. How can we help our daughter to accept praise with a meek and quiet spirit?

_____

_____

_____

## Building a Relationship of Love and Respect

9. What activities help to build a relationship of love and respect between a mother and daughter?

_____

_____

_____

10. Suppose your daughter wants a dollhouse. Why is it usually better to make one together than to buy one at a store?

_____

_____

_____

11. How does firmness and consistency in disciplining a daughter help to build a relationship of love and respect?

_____

_____

_____

12. Suppose a daughter comes running with a handful of flowers, but her mother says, "Those are just dandelions!" What is the result?

_____

_____

_____

13. How should we handle confidential matters that our daughters share with us?

_____

_____

_____

14. How can we maintain a heroine image in our daughter's eyes?

_____

_____

_____

## To Serve, Not Be Served

15. Describe the basic concept of Christian servanthood.

_____

_____

16. What are some practical evidences of having an attitude of servanthood?

_____

_____

_____

17. How can we make the concept of serving others a familiar experience for our daughters?

_____

_____

_____

## What About a Vocation?

18. When our daughters want to do something more than cooking, cleaning, and sewing, what are some good options to consider?

_____

_____

_____

19. What are some dangers in letting our daughters work in non-Christian environments?

_____

_____

_____

20. What voluntary service opportunities are available for our daughters?

_____

_____

_____

21. Why is it especially valuable for our daughters to work for other families in the church?

_____

_____

_____

## Single Daughters Away From Home

22. What values learned in her own home help to prepare a daughter for getting along well in someone else's home?

_____

_____

23. Single daughters living away from home face what challenge in relation to headship?

_____

_____

_____

24. Why is it safest for a single daughter away from home to receive counsel from several men?

_____

_____

_____

## Guiding Them Through Courtship

25. During courtship, what is more important than pursuing the courtship itself?

_____

_____

_____

26. What must our daughter remember about those younger than she?

_____

_____

27. What advice will help our daughter to control her thoughts?

_____

_____

_____

## Ideals for Their Future Husbands

28. What requirement must always be foremost in considering a potential husband?

_____

_____

_____

29. What are some other important ideals to look for in a young man who asks our daughter for her friendship?

_____

_____

_____

## Some of a Mother's Responsibilities

30. How should we guard our daughter's associations with boys before she is old enough to begin courtship?

_____

_____

_____

31. How can a mother help her daughter to accept the possibility of a single life?

_____

_____

_____

32. When is the best time to evaluate a young man who asks for a daughter's friendship? What should the daughter do in deciding how to respond?

_____

_____

_____

33. How should parents be involved in their daughter's courtship right from the beginning?

_____

_____

_____

34. How is physical touch a threat to pure courtship?

_____

_____

_____

35. What warning should be given about soft and sentimental speech and actions?

_____

_____

_____

36. What are some wholesome activities for a daughter's courtship visits?

_____

_____

_____

## Engagement and Marriage

37. How is the engagement period a time of relinquishing control of a daughter's life?

_____

_____

_____

38. How is a daughter's wedding both a sad and a joyful occasion?

_____

_____

_____

## Consider further:

How do you suppose your daughters evaluate your mothering skills?

### Home to Mother

Where are you going, my little lass,
Girl in your teens, . . . young lady now?
Where are you going, my woman grown,
With a babe in your arms to call your own?
She answered sweetly, "Don't you know?
No matter how old or tired we grow,
No one has ever yet moved slow
When going home to Mother."

—Ada L. Wine

# Chapter 19

# Relating to Our Sons

My son—a trust from God.
My son—to be linked to the greater world around him.
My son—today a smiling, trusting toddler;
   Tomorrow, a man for God's glory,
   We hope and pray he will be.

A trust from God is a weighty matter because He expects us to order our child in godly ways. Raising a son is a serious responsibility. It is an awesome and often overwhelming responsibility to provide for his physical and spiritual needs. He will be the product of our home.

## Teaching Them to Work

1. Since work is a necessity, what attitudes should our sons learn in relation to it?

   _____

   _____

   _____

2. How can we help our sons to be diligent workers?

   _____

   _____

   _____

3. How is work a discipline for our sons?

   _____

   _____

   _____

4. How can we help our sons to gain confidence in their abilities?

   _____

   _____

## Guiding Them in Their Work With Others

5. How should our son relate to his employer?

   _____

   _____

   _____

6. What are some principles for parents to remember as they seek a job for their son?

   _____

   _____

   _____

7. What is harmful about letting our sons spend money for all kinds of gadgets?

   _____

   _____

   _____

8. How should our son relate to other employees?

   _____

   _____

   _____

## A Proper Relationship With Father

9. Why is it important for our son to have a proper image of Father?

   _____

   _____

10. How can a mother best help her son to respect and honor Father?

   _____

   _____

   _____

11. What position and responsibility does Father have, for which he deserves respect?

   _____

   _____

12. How can you help a good relationship to develop between your husband and a new son?

_____

_____

_____

13. How can you encourage the continuing development of a good relationship between your husband and your son?

_____

_____

14. How can you help your son to respect Father in spite of his weaknesses?

_____

_____

_____

## Polishing Their Character

15. Since polishing is primarily Father's role, what is Mother's contribution?

_____

_____

_____

16. What will help our sons to be victorious over the carnal nature?

_____

_____

17. What do boys reveal when they tease younger ones or become boastful and condescending? What can mothers do about this?

_____

_____

_____

## Preparing Them to Take Up the Mantle

18. What does it mean to "take up the mantle"?

_____

_____

19. What are some things that prepare a son to take up the mantle?

_____

_____

_____

20. How does an active devotional life improve a young man's character? How does it help him to be a fruitful worker in the church?

_____

_____

_____

_____

21. How does a young man show that he has a workable spirit rather than an independent spirit?

_____

_____

_____

22. How can you tell whether your son is ready to lead a wife and family?

_____

_____

## Guiding Him Through Courtship and Marriage

23. A son should be able to say, "I want a wife like my mother." How can his mother be worthy of that?

_____

_____

_____

24. In what ways should a son be the leader in courtship?

_____

_____

_____

_____

25. What is the parents' primary role as they watch their son go through the engagement period and enter marriage?

_____

_____

_____

## Consider further:

Name several ways that your relationship to your husband affects your training of your sons.

May a mother's prayers follow each son as he leaves home:

> "Be with him, Lord, tonight;
>     Protect him on his way;
> Give wisdom, courage, strength;
>     Direct each future day.
> Help him to learn the tasks
>     That seem at first so strange;
> Guard when temptations come,
>     Lest his convictions change."
> —*Ada L. Wine*

# Chapter 20

# The Married Child

Still hand in hand, their journey through,
Joint pilgrims may they go;
Mingling their joys as helpers true,
And sharing every woe.

*—William Gaskell*

## A New Family Unit

1. In what ways can we promote good relationships with our married child and spouse?

_____

_____

_____

_____

_____

_____

2. How should we relate to the mistakes of a son-in-law or daughter-in-law?

_____

_____

_____

3. Suggest some practical ways of being a witness to non-Christian married children.

_____

_____

_____

_____

## Grandmother–Grandchildren Relationships

4. What are grandparents tempted to think when they see negative traits in their grandchildren? What truth should they recognize?

_____

_____

_____

5. How can a grandmother relate to her grandchildren in ways that strengthen the tie between herself and their parents?

_____

_____

_____

6. What are some benefits of baby-sitting by Grandmother?

_____

_____

_____

7. Why might baby-sitting become stressful for Grandmother?

_____

_____

_____

8. How should an adopted grandchild be treated?

_____

_____

_____

## How We Can Help

9. Why is it important to pray daily for our married children and the grandchildren? What should we pray for?

_____

_____

_____

10. How can we show love and respect to our married child and his or her spouse?

    _____

    _____

    _____

11. What are some pointers for giving advice?

    _____

    _____

    _____

12. What is involved in showing impartiality to all the children and grandchildren?

    _____

    _____

    _____

## Supporting Their Efforts

13. Why do our married children need to hear the message "Be strong and of good courage"?

    _____

    _____

    _____

14. How might mothers and grandmothers hinder their married children who are called to serve the Lord in a distant place? What should they do instead?

    _____

    _____

    _____

    _____

    _____

    _____

## Consider further:

What do you think is or will be your greatest strength as you relate to your married children, in-laws, and grandchildren? your greatest weakness?

# Chapter 21

# Mother, an Example in Purity

Mothers care about purity—
> Untainted food,
> Clean wounds,
> Pure drinking water,
> And freedom from sin and guilt.

## Proper Attitudes

1. Why does a discussion of purity begin with proper attitudes?

2. How can we fortify ourselves against temptation?

3. How might we be deceived into tolerating impurity?

4. What are some results of feeding on impure things?

5. How can we start an upward spiral for our posterity?

6. Why is it dangerous to say, "That doesn't bother me"?

# A Mother Displaying Proper Reserve

7. What is involved in displaying proper reserve?

_____

_____

_____

8. Why should a woman be careful not to touch a man other than her husband?

_____

_____

_____

9. What are some ways to avoid giving the appearance of evil?

_____

_____

_____

_____

_____

10. What are some reasons for dressing modestly?

_____

_____

_____

# Showing Reserve in Public

11. What are some actions that a woman should avoid while in public?

_____

_____

_____

12. How can we let our eyes "look right on" when we go shopping or to town?

_____

_____

_____

13. What are some friendly actions that are safe for a woman?

_____

_____

## Showing Reserve in Our Homes

14. What can we do at home to teach reserve to our children?

_____

_____

_____

15. How can we clearly show our children that we love their father, while still maintaining a proper reserve?

_____

_____

_____

## The Christian Salutation

16. What are the appropriate Biblical salutations for Christians? What are some inappropriate salutations?

_____

_____

_____

_____

17. What can we do to minimize the chances of an unwanted hug?

_____

_____

## Relating to Sincere Seekers

18. What danger might be posed by a seeking man who is divorced or has no family?

_____

_____

_____

19. What is a safe way for a wife to relate to a man who is a seeker?

_____

_____

_____

## A Mother Showing Improper Reserve

20. For what reasons might a mother be caught in things that show improper reserve?

_____

_____

_____

21. How might a mother show improper reserve by what she wears? by the use of her voice?

_____

_____

_____

22. What activities might endanger the spiritual life of a Christian woman?

_____

_____

_____

## Consider further:

What new thoughts, or old thoughts anew, came to your mind as you read this chapter?

Purer in heart, O God,
Help me to be;
That I Thy holy face
One day may see.
—*Mrs. A. L. Davison*

**Chapter 22**

# Guarding Our Children's Innocence

Even a child is known by his doings,
whether his work be pure, and whether it be right.
Proverbs 20:11

We live in a wicked world. Before the Flood, God saw that every imagination of man's heart was only evil continually. It is no better today.

Take a look at your baby. How pure and spotless he is! Oh, that we could keep him that way! We need to guard his purity with all diligence as he enters our wicked world.

## Teaching Them About Modesty

1. How does teaching reserve and modesty to a child help to guard his innocence?

_____

_____

_____

2. What are some specific points of modesty that children should be taught?

_____

_____

_____

## Answering Their Questions

3. What are some good ways to answer little children who ask, "Where do babies come from?"

_____

_____

_____

4. What are some guidelines for giving more specific answers to such questions?

_____

_____

_____

## The Things They See and Hear

5. Though we seek to protect our children, what are some sources through which they may be exposed to evil?

_____

_____

6. What should we do if we hear a child using inappropriate words?

_____

_____

_____

7. How should we respond if our children imitate the sensual actions of others?

_____

_____

_____

8. Why should children not be allowed to read romance stories?

_____

_____

_____

9. What should we do when our children see improperly dressed people in public?

_____

_____

_____

10. What are some signs that a child may have been exposed to evil and is hiding it?

_____

_____

_____

11. How can we encourage our children to tell us things that bother them?

## Safe Friends

12. What are some things about children that we should remember when we visit trusted friends and relatives?

13. How can we discreetly monitor children's activities whether at home or visiting elsewhere?

## Monitoring Their Play

14. What are some safeguards that will help to protect our children's innocence during play?

15. Too much idle time will bring undue temptations to children. How can we counteract this?

*16. Discuss how a child's purity is affected by each of the following: playmates, books and magazines, music, games, toys

## Children Learn Things on Their Own

17.  When we see evil in our child, why must we not assume that it is due to some outside influence?

    _____

    _____

18.  Jesus said, "I pray not that thou shouldest take them out of the world, but that thou shouldest keep them from the evil" (John 17:15). How does this relate to child training?

    _____

    _____

## Consider further:

How can you guard the purity of your children without stirring improper anxiety or curiosity?

# Chapter 23

# Adoption

Who knoweth whether thou art come to the kingdom
for such a time as this?
Esther 4:14
God's call of service for you may be to minister to a child not born to you.

## Some Obstacles We Face

1. Following are some common objections to adopting children. What are some good responses to them?

   a. "You don't know what kind of 'blood' you will bring into your home or the church."

   _____

   _____

   b. "Adopted children often do not turn out well."

   _____

   _____

   c. "What will this do to your *own* children?"

   _____

   _____

2. How can parents gain the confidence they need to adopt a child?

   _____

   _____

   _____

## When to Think of Adoption

3. When a woman is barren, what are some things she is commonly tempted to think?

   _____

   _____

   _____

4. What are some positive ways to respond to barrenness?

_____

_____

_____

5. How can natural mothers show consideration to women who are barren?

_____

_____

_____

6. What other than barrenness may be reasons to consider adoption?

_____

_____

_____

_____

7. How is adoption a form of evangelization?

_____

_____

_____

## Adoption Is Voluntary

8. In what sense is an adopted child more special than a natural child?

_____

_____

## His Privileges

9. In what ways does an adopted child have the same privileges as a natural child?

_____

_____

_____

_____

10. In trying to make an adopted child feel loved and accepted, what mistake can parents easily make in relation to obedience?

_____

_____

11. Sometimes an adopted child receives more spankings than a natural child, and he thinks it is because he is adopted. How can you show him that you are not being partial?

_____

_____

_____

## The Adopted Child Needs Us

12. In what ways should an adopted child be challenged by his parents?

_____

_____

_____

13. Why might an adopted child need extra support?

_____

_____

_____

## Dealing With Rejection and Loss

14. What is the basic reason that an adopted child must deal with rejection and loss?

_____

_____

_____

15. What are the advantages of adopting a baby over adopting an older child?

_____

_____

_____

16. What are some problems that parents face in adopting an older child?

_____

_____

_____

17. How can we break down the barriers between us and a grieving, adopted child?

_____

_____

_____

18. If a child was adopted as a baby, when and how should we tell him about it?

_____

_____

_____

_____

19. How is love for someone else's child different from love for one's own child? What must adoptive parents be careful to do because of this fact?

_____

_____

_____

## We Need Our Adopted Child

20. What blessings do our adopted children provide in the present and in the future?

_____

_____

_____

_____

21. What need can our adopted children fill in relation to the Lord's work?

_____

_____

_____

## When Others Relate to Our Child

22. Why do older children sometimes keep their distance from a child who is "different"?

   _____

   _____

   _____

23. People sometimes make unkind remarks about a child we have adopted.
   a. How should we respond when we hear such remarks?

   _____

   _____

   b. How should we *not* respond? Why not?

   _____

   _____

   _____

24. How can we show unfailing love to an adopted child?

   _____

   _____

## Blending Our Family

25. What is the key to blending natural children and adopted children into one unified family?

   _____

   _____

   _____

26. In what ways can parents promote this kind of blending?

   _____

   _____

   _____

## Consider further:

Does this chapter challenge any of your ideas about what it is like to have an adopted child?

**Chapter 24**

# The Special Child

"O man, who art thou that repliest against God? Shall the thing formed say to him that formed it, Why hast thou made me thus?" (Romans 9:20). Should a created being question his Creator? Dare we do that?

Our God is infinite, which means He has no limitations and boundaries. In our wildest imagination, we could not fancy the scope of that idea. God can do whatever He pleases. Yet He is concerned about me, one who is only a particle of the nations that "are as a drop of a bucket" (Isaiah 40:15). He has a plan for my life and a plan for your life. Surely we can place our hands in His and trust His wisdom.

For me to remember: As I fear God, He guides my life in a plan of His own making.

## "Who Hath Made . . ."

1. What truths must we be convinced of, regardless of the condition of a special child?

   _____

   _____

   _____

2. Describe contrasting ways in which a special child could be treated, and the results of each.

   _____

   _____

   _____

   _____

3. What lessons can a special child help us to learn? How might he contribute to God's glory?

   _____

   _____

   _____

## Accepting My Responsibility

4. When a special child is born, what are some typical responses of the mother?

 

 

5. What thoughts will help such a mother to rise above her fears?

 

 

6. How can such a mother find strength to care for all the members in her family?

 

 

7. Why is acceptance of a special child not a once-and-done experience?

 

 

8. How might such a mother's contentment with her lot be a help to someone else?

 

 

## Living With Our Child

9. What can a mother do to provide a peaceful environment for a special child?

 

 

 

10. In measuring a special child's progress, what are some good comparisons to make? What are some poor comparisons?

_____

_____

_____

11. What kind of discipline does a special child need?

_____

_____

_____

12. What should a mother do when she cannot control the annoying habits of a special child?

_____

_____

_____

## How Others Can Help

13. How can other mothers be a blessing to the mother of a special child?

_____

_____

_____

14. What can you do to show your acceptance of a special child in your church?

_____

_____

_____

15. What should normal children be taught in relation to children with special needs?

_____

_____

_____

## Consider further:

What suggestions from your personal observations can you add to this chapter?

# Chapter 25

# Trials and Afflictions

Beneath His watchful eye
His saints securely dwell;
That hand which bears all nature up
Shall guard His children well.
                    —*Philip Doddridge*

One summer we had plenty of sunshine and the crops grew well—at first. But with the sun shining day after day, the crops started hankering for rain. The lawns turned brown and brittle. The sunshine was good, but it was not all we needed. We needed rain for crops to grow and for lawns to turn green.

For us to prosper spiritually, we need diversity in our Christian lives. We need adversity along with times of prosperity. As we walk with God day after day, we want to be conscious of His watchful eye over us, knowing that He is preparing the way for us.

## Reasons for Trials and Afflictions

1. What are some reasons for trials and afflictions?

2. What are some temptations that we must guard against when trials and afflictions come?

3. What attitudes will help us to "come forth as gold" after a trial?

4. What can trials teach us?

_____

_____

5. What truths from the Bible will help to make afflictions and chastening more bearable?

_____

_____

_____

_____

## Our Response to Trials and Afflictions

6. What is the right choice to make in response to trials and afflictions?

_____

_____

7. Describe some wrong responses to afflictions, along with their results.

_____

_____

_____

8. What are some expressions of discouragement? some results?

_____

_____

_____

9. What are we implying when we question God's wisdom in allowing trials?

_____

_____

_____

10. What are some expressions that reveal acceptance of God's plan in trials?

_____

_____

_____

11. What is meant by being "patient in tribulation"?

_____

_____

12. How can we be thankful even after the death of a loved one?

_____

_____

## The Mother's Help

13. From each Scripture below, give a fact that is a special comfort in affliction.

    a. "The angel of the LORD encampeth round about them that fear him, and delivereth them."

    _____

    _____

    b. "My help cometh from the LORD, which made heaven and earth."

    _____

    _____

    c. "[He] comforteth us in all our tribulation."

    _____

    _____

    d. "Fear thou not; for I am with thee: be not dismayed; for I am thy God."

    _____

    _____

14. Explain how comfort from God can have a domino effect.

_____

_____

## Consider further:

Can you think of reasons why God would allow affliction in your life other than to purge something evil out of your character?

# Chapter 26

# Mothering Alone

He leadeth me: O blessed thought!
O words with heavenly comfort fraught!
Whate'er I do, where'er I be,
Still 'tis God's hand that leadeth me.
—*Joseph H. Gilmore*

## Mothering Alone Is Not Our Choice

1. Why can widowhood rightly be called an affliction?

<br><br>

## God's Provisions

2. In what ways is God a husband to a widow?

<br><br>

3. What is the benefit of the Spirit's intercession for a widow?

<br><br>

4. How does God provide for a widow through brethren and sisters in the church?

<br><br><br>

5. What comfort lies in the fact that the Lord stands as Judge for the widow's cause?

<br><br><br>

## God's Directions for Us

6. A good therapy for grief is activity. What are some ways that a widow can keep busy?

   _____

   _____

   _____

   _____

7. How should a wife relate to the church after she becomes a widow?

   _____

   _____

8. Why is a widow well qualified to relieve the afflicted?

   _____

   _____

   _____

9. What services can a widow perform regardless of age or poverty?

   _____

   _____

   _____

## Taking the Leadership Role

10. What should be a widow's primary concern when taking the leadership role? What is involved in this?

    _____

    _____

11. Why should a widow not make all her decisions alone? Where can she find help with this?

    _____

    _____

    _____

12. What are some pointers for maintaining family worship?

    _____

    _____

    _____

13. How can a widow provide the father-touch that her children need?

_____

_____

_____

_____

14. Why does it usually not work to have another friend or relative take the leadership role in a widow's family?

_____

_____

15. In what undesirable ways may older children show their grief at the loss of Father? How should their mother respond?

_____

_____

_____

## When to Be Open to Another Relationship

16. Why does a widow often prefer to remain single? What may prepare her for another relationship?

_____

_____

_____

17. When a widow considers another relationship, under what circumstances should the children's needs take precedence?

_____

_____

## When We Need to Work for a Living

18. How can families in the church reduce the stress of a single mother who must work to support her family?

_____

_____

_____

_____

19. When a working mother has a day off to be with her children, how should she spend the day?

_____

_____

_____

_____

20. What is the result when a working mother allows God to perform His work in her life?

_____

_____

_____

## Consider further:

How can a widow include other men in her family life while still observing propriety?

# Chapter 27

# Money Matters

Take heed, and beware of covetousness:
for a man's life consisteth not
in the abundance of the things which he possesseth.
Luke 12:15

1. In providing an income, a husband may deal with unpleasant things that a wife seldom has to face. What are some of these?

   _____

   _____

   _____

2. What is meant by the saying that a woman can throw things out the back door with a spoon faster than a man can bring them in the front door with a shovel?

   _____

   _____

   _____

3. What problems are commonly caused by credit card buying?

   _____

   _____

   _____

4. What can we do to make frugal use of the food and clothing we have?

   _____

   _____

   _____

   _____

5. Some people try to increase their income to match their spending. What is a better approach?

_____

_____

_____

6. Why is our good stewardship important in relation to our children?

_____

_____

## Consider further:

When you talk about finances with your husband, which point of discussion most often causes tension? What can you do to improve on this point?

# Chapter 28

# As We Grow Older

In our older years, goals keep our minds focused on the important things in life. But as much as we would like to keep plowing ahead as we did in younger years, our physical bodies may say, "Slow down!" We may be able to keep the same goals but work toward them at a slower pace. Some goals may need to be exchanged for others.

We want to maintain our spiritual life even if we are immobilized and unable to work. At the end of life, we want to say with the apostle Paul, "I have fought a good fight, I have finished my course, I have kept the faith: henceforth there is laid up for me a crown of righteousness" (2 Timothy 4:7, 8).

## "Though Our Outward Man Perish"

1. What negative factor is commonly associated with growing older?

   _____

   _____

## Strength Through Faith

2. How is Abraham's wife Sarah an encouragement to us about the challenges of senior years?

   _____

   _____

   _____

3. What are some things in old age for which we need the strength that comes by faith?

   _____

   _____

   _____

4. How does a shared vision of the Lord's work contribute to a good relationship between husband and wife?

   _____

   _____

   _____

5. What are some things to remember about fighting the enemy of our souls?

   _____

   _____

   _____

   _____

## "A Restorer of Thy Life"

6. In relating to Ruth and Boaz, how is Naomi a good example for us?

   _____

   _____

   _____

7. How does God continue to provide for us in our old age?

   _____

   _____

   _____

8. If you are an older person, how have your grandchildren and great-grandchildren been "a restorer of thy life"?

   _____

   _____

9. In what ways can an older person bless the lives of children and of adults?

   _____

   _____

   _____

   _____

   _____

10. What can faithful grandparents expect to see, which will make them feel that their lives have been extended and rewarded? What makes this result possible?

_____

_____

_____

_____

## Consider further:

What qualities in older women have you admired that you would like to imitate?